Chinese **mao**

Danish **miav**

French **miaou**

Finnish **miau, kurnau**

German **miau**

Dutch **miauw**

Catalan **meu**

Swedish **mjau**

Hebrew **miau** and sometimes **miya**

me

what **CATS** are made of

ow'

what **cats**

are made of by hanoch piven

ginee seo books

Atheneum Books for Young Readers

New York London Toronto Sydney

To Paddy, Smurf, Vanunu,
and Crudo, long-gone
to Cat Heaven

Atheneum Books for Young Readers
An imprint of Simon & Schuster
Children's Publishing Division
1230 Avenue of the Americas
New York, New York 10020
Copyright © 2009 by Hanoch Piven
All rights reserved, including the
right of reproduction in whole or in
part in any form.
Book design by Ann Bobco
Photography by Cristina Reche
The text for this book is set in
Filosofia, Dalliance, and Gill Sans.
The illustrations for this book
are collages mixed with digital
backgrounds.
Manufactured in China
First Edition
10 9 8 7 6 5 4 3 2 1
CIP data for this book is available
from the Library of Congress.
ISBN-13: 978-1-4169-1531-7
ISBN-10: 1-4169-1531-1

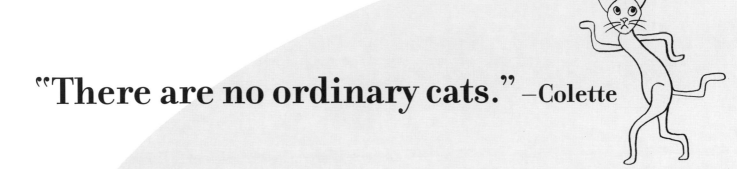

"There are no ordinary cats." –Colette

There are thirty-nine registered breeds of cats.
Some are short, some are long, some are skinny,
and some are fat. Some are playful and some are
quiet, and some love people and some even act like
dogs! Cats are made of all kinds of things. But
there's one thing they have in common: They are
special, and they know it. Because as Leonardo
da Vinci said, "The smallest feline is a masterpiece."

cats are made of energy

The Devon rex is such a mischievous cat that it's been compared to a monkey. These curly haired cats love to jump and have been found climbing brick fireplaces and perching atop doors, closets, shelves—even the occasional laundry basket. They are accomplished food moochers, so watch that bag of snack food on the kitchen table—or before you know it, you'll find a Devon rex grazing contentedly inside it.

Feline Fact: Cats usually land on their feet when they fall because of what's known as a "cat righting reflex." Due to their flexibility and sense of balance, they are able to right themselves in the air—provided they have enough time. A cat can jump five times the length of its tail.

cats are made of glamour

Persian cats are the models of the cat world. Famously elegant and expressive, they love to pose and will drape themselves by a favorite window or in a chair for hours, which makes them a favorite of photographers and advertisers. Even their origins are glamorous: It's said that they came to the west from Persia and Iran, smuggled among rare spices and jewels on basket-laden camels.

Feline Fact: Cats can't taste sugary foods. Scientists believe this may be due to a defect in a key taste receptor.

cats are made of
toughness

Many people believe that Siberian cats make very good guards. It's said that they, along with monks, guarded monasteries in Russia, so if you own a Siberian, you might notice that it'll let you know when a visitor is coming to your house. Siberians are extremely agile and can leap great distances and heights without breaking bric-a-brac. But you still might want to put away that expensive vase if there's one around.

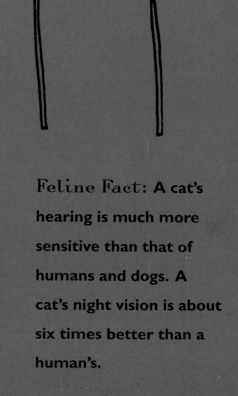

Feline Fact: A cat's hearing is much more sensitive than that of humans and dogs. A cat's night vision is about six times better than a human's.

cats are made of
origami

Scottish Fold cats have ears that are folded forward and down onto their heads, just like their origami versions! The folded ears are produced by an incomplete gene and are the result of a mutation. Not all Scottish Fold cats have folded ears, but all of them carry the gene for this characteristic. In fact, Scottish Fold kittens are born with normal ears. At about three to four weeks of age, their ears fold . . . or not!

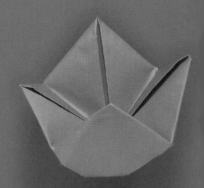

Feline Fact: Cats have thirty-two muscles that control the outer ear (humans have only six). A cat can independently rotate his ears 180 degrees.

cats are made of
brains

The Siamese are among the most intelligent cats and also among the most loving. Their need for human companionship may have evolved as a survival trait. Because of their distinctive markings, the Siamese coat is ineffective as camouflage. They are a breed that is able to communicate with humans like no other. The voice of the Siamese is legendary, as you can find out for yourself when you're taking care of a Siamese that wants something from you!

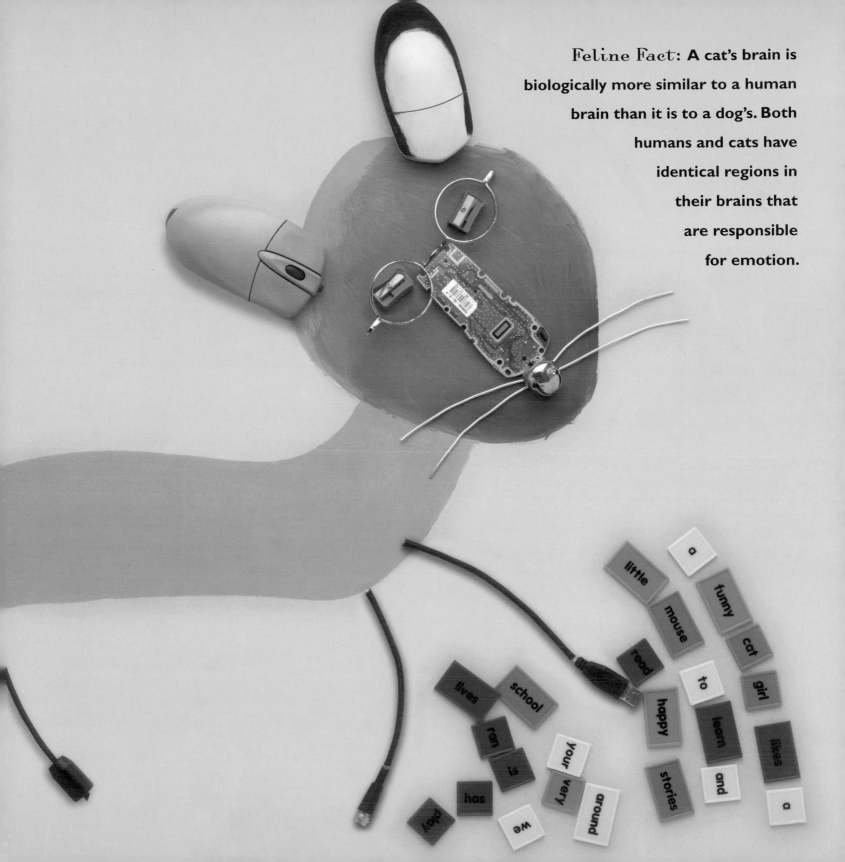

Feline Fact: A cat's brain is biologically more similar to a human brain than it is to a dog's. Both humans and cats have identical regions in their brains that are responsible for emotion.

cats are made of

laziness

The Exotic Shorthair cat looks a lot like a Persian cat with short hair. It also looks a lot like a football linebacker with its large head; short, thick neck; medium to large body; large forehead; and small ears and nose. These cats are known as "the lazy man's Persian," because their short hair makes them easy to groom. Exotics are extremely affectionate. Some will sit on your shoulder and hug you when you pet them!

Feline Fact: Cats nap—a lot! The average cat sleeps about thirteen to fourteen hours a day.

cats are made of
guts

Most cats are afraid of water, but not the **Savannah**. This cat will play in it and even dunk itself in it! This is a cat that behaves very much like a dog—it can be trained to walk on a leash and even fetch. Savannahs often like to greet people with a head butt or a pounce. The Savannah's wild-looking appearance and behavior is due to the fact that it is descended from a domestic cat and a wild African serval.

Feline Fact:
Cats walk on their toes. They move both left legs and then both right legs when they walk or run. A domestic cat can sprint thirty-one miles an hour!

cats are made of legends

There are several wild stories about the origins of the Maine coon cat, one of the oldest natural breeds in North America. According to one legend, the first Maine coon was the offspring of a domestic cat and a raccoon! (This is biologically impossible.) Another legend says the breed came from six cats Marie Antoinette sent to Maine when she was planning to escape France during the French Revolution. Some breeders believe that they may be descended from cats the Vikings brought to America.

Maine coons are playful and very dexterous, especially with their front paws, which they use to open cabinet doors, turn on water faucets, or pick up small objects. Some Maine coons will even eat from their paws instead of their bowls!

Feline Fact:
A cat's jaw moves only up and down, not side to side, like dogs and humans. When a cat drinks, its tongue, which has tiny rear-pointing barbs on it, scoops up the liquid and collects enough water at the back of its throat to swallow.

cats are made of
showbiz

The British Shorthair cat is the actor of the cat world. Calm, loyal, and intelligent, this breed is so well behaved and easy to discipline that it has become the favorite of animal trainers in Hollywood, and many British Shorthairs appear in films and television shows. The British Shorthair is probably the oldest breed of English cat and traces its ancestry all the way back to the domestic cat of Rome.

cats are made of
mutations

The Sphynx looks like a cat without hair! In 1966 a domestic cat in Toronto, Canada, gave birth to a hairless kitten. This mystery of nature was a naturally occurring mutation, and a new breed of cat was born. Sphynx cats actually do have hair, but it is so fine and downy that the animals look hairless. And they do get cold, so you should definitely dress your Sphynx in a sweater during the winter!

Feline Fact:
The normal body temperature of a cat is between 100.5° and 102.5° F. A cat is sick if its temperature goes below 100° or above 103° F.

cats are made of softness

The Ragdoll cat got its name from the fact that many cats in this breed go completely limp and relaxed when they are picked up—just like rag dolls. These cats are some of the gentlest and easiest to live with, and they love being around people. In fact, there is a Ragdoll cat named Matilda who has lived for eleven years in the Algonquin Hotel, where she is free to go anywhere she wants—except for the kitchen! Matilda even has her own e-mail address: matildaalgonquincat@algonquinhotel.com.

Feline Fact: **A cat has two hundred and thirty bones in its body (humans have two hundred and six). A cat has no collarbone, so it can fit through any opening the size of its head (unless it's an extremely fat cat, of course!)**

Feline Fact:
Cats don't really
have nine lives, but
they do tend to
live a long time—
from fourteen to
twenty years. The
oldest known cat
lived to the age of
thirty-six!

cats are made of
history

The **Abyssinian** cat is an acrobat and troublemaker and loves to be the center of attention. These cats resemble the paintings and sculptures of the cats of ancient Egypt, and one story has it that they originate from a kitten brought to England from Egypt by a British soldier.

A few superstitions

Every cat has **nine lives**.

If a black cat crosses your path, you will have **bad luck**. (In England, however, the bad luck can be canceled if you spit right away.)

If you wake up in the morning and see cats playing, the rest of the day **will be wasted**.

A strange black cat on your porch **brings prosperity**.

A cat sneezing is a **good omen** for everyone who hears it.

A cat sleeping with all four paws tucked under means **cold weather ahead**.

If a cat sneezes near a bride-to-be on the morning of the wedding, she will have a **happy life**.

about cats

If cats run around wildly, then **expect a wind to blow up**.

If a cat washes behind its ears, **it will rain**.

A three-colored cat will keep the house **safe from fire**.

If you dream of a multicolored cat, you will have **luck making friends**.

If you pay money for a cat, it will **never catch mice** for you.

If a cat is dreaming, pull a whisker from its lip, sleep on it that night, and **you will dream** what the cat was dreaming.

Letting a cat look into a mirror will cause you **trouble**.

"A cat's a cat and that's that." —American folk saying

Korean
yaong or nyaong

Hungarian
miau

English
meow

Norwegian
mjau

Portuguese
miau

Japanese
nyan, nyaa

Spanish
miau

Greek
naiou